# COLLEGE IN A NUTSKULL

## 17½ SUBJECTS

## A Crash~ED~ Course in Higher Education

COMPILED & EDITED BY
PROFESSOR ANDERS
HENRIKSSON

To the memory of V.J. Brown and

Ralph Sherrard—friends, collaborators,

and connoisseurs of student wit.

Library of Congress Cataloging-in-Publication Data is available.

ISBN 978-0-7611-5465-5

Design by Jen Browning
Cover design by David Matt

Workman books are available at special discounts when purchased in bulk for premiums and sales promotions as well as for fund-raising or educational use. Special editions or book excerpts also can be created to specification. For details, contact the Special Sales Director at the address below.

Workman Publishing Company, Inc.
225 Varick Street
New York, NY 10014-4381
www.workman.com

Printed in the United States of America
First printing February 2010

10 9 8 7 6 5 4 3 2 1

# CONTENTS

## INTRODUCTION

The creative imagination of college students is wondrous to behold. After nearly forty years in the classroom, I continue to marvel at their captivating and certifiably unique insights into the world around us. Who could ever become bored or jaded reading about Shakespeare winning the Nobel Prize or the adventures of bold explorers like Vasco Iguana? Students in my history classes at Shepherd University remain a source of delightful insights into both past and present. The years since the appearance of *Ignorance Is Blitz* (originally published as *Non Campus Mentis*) have seen exponential growth in the network of friends and colleagues who kindly supply me with material from their own students. They include not only fellow historians, but also linguists, musicologists, psychologists, art historians, biologists, physicists, sociologists, political scientists, economists, mathematicians, scholars of literature, and others.

My unwitting (and mercifully anonymous) student collaborators represent a spectrum of institutions, large and small, public and private, from across America. There is also a substantial contribution from Australia, Canada, and New Zealand. Almost all of the material comes from essays and examination papers, but there are some other sources. Course evaluation forms can provide a startling glimpse into the undergraduate mind. Today's plugged-in generation is also far from shy about texting, phoning, and e-mailing their professors; and I have mined this material as well.

The prose in this volume belongs entirely to the students. My contribution is minimal. I have organized the material into a study guide by subject. And in some cases I have actually corrected spelling that was so murky that it obscured the underlying humor.

I am often asked if my compilations of creative inanity point to a dark future shrouded in ignorance. Are latter-day Visigoths running amok through the halls of ivy? Undergraduate education certainly faces some daunting challenges. More than a few students arrive on campus unable to express themselves in clear English. Professors can take little for granted even when it comes to the most basic understanding of geography, history, natural science, or how one's own country is governed. In recent years I have also encountered a growing number of students whose high school experience seems to have included a lot of drilling for standardized tests. Some freshmen are discombobulated by exams in other formats and by the absence of a dry run or two. Technology is a two-edged sword. It opens avenues of inquiry, enhances the classroom environment, and offers ready access to a stunning wealth of information. Yet it also shreds attention spans and tempts young minds with a salad bar of distractions. The student who appears to be intently taking notes on a laptop may actually be surfing the net. Omnipresent iPods and cell phones can cloak students in a cocoon of self-absorption. I am amazed at the ability of some to take notes with a pen in one hand while using the other to text on a cell phone concealed under the desk.

These are all serious issues, but a wider perspective presents a somewhat more reassuring picture. When have students not slipped into daydreams during class, failed to study for an exam, or dashed off a term paper during a frantic all-nighter? The malapropisms, blunders, and skewed associations which comprise this book represent a tiny fragment of the student writing that my faculty contributors and I have read over the years. For every student who thinks that Egypt is an island or that the U.S. Congress is prohibited from making laws, there are scores of well-informed, articulate undergraduates eager to learn. Really!

My advice? Cast aside all worry and savor this text as an opportunity to visit a world remarkably different from the reality we think we inhabit.

# Religious Studies

## Bananas from Heaven

GOD MADE THE WATERS AND THEN FIRMED UP THE

PERMANENT. THIS, AT ANY RATE, IS WHAT HE HAD TO

SAY IN THE BIBLE, WHICH WAS HIS ONE

AND ONLY NOVEL.

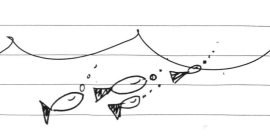

## HOLY SPIN

The Book of Geniuses tells the story of Adam and Eve in the Garden of Eaton. Everyone was happy until they gave in to the ideas of the local wildlife. Eve ate the holy fig leaf. This led to original spin. An angry God made them go camping.

MAJOR POINTS

✳ God gave Moses the Bill of Rights.

✳ Captain Ahab became King of Isreal.

The Hebrew people were very unhappy in Eygpt because Fharo would not allow them to celebrate Easter. Moses led his Islams out of Egypt. Bananas from heaven arrived to feed the hungry people. These events are described in the Book of Zeus.

The sayings of Jesus are contained in the Analects. These include, "Let them who have not sinned be first to get stoned," and, "You cannot serve both God and Manhattan."

Jesus was born in swaggering clothes. Thus did God send us his only forgotten son. Even today Jesus has a lot of importance in Christianity.

KEY BELIEFS

＊Christianity gradually developed a
   monotheistic deity for easier worship.

＊The Nicene Creed required everyone to
   be nice to each other.

＊Monasteries were a place to expatriate
   your sins. The Rule of St. Benedict forbid
   the use of clothing in the monastery.

THE FIRST PART OF THE BIBLE IS KNOWN AS "THE PENTAGON," BECAUSE IT HAS A LOT OF WAR IN IT.

✳ The church sentenced nuns to claustrophobia. This required a life of celery.

During the Middle Ages church and state were not only in bed together, but went way beyond just hugging and kissing. Gregory VII was a Pope who desired more power and larger personal ornaments. One of his acts was to abolish women.

Luther, who became aroused when the
Catholics began to sell repugnances in
his home town, denounced the Church
for its sin and ubiquity. The Diet of Worms
was Luther's punishment for starting the
Reformation.

The Spanish Inquisition was where people
were asked questions about Spanish
culture.

For the most part, Calvin was against sin.
His restrictions on drinking and dancing on
Sunday led to the birth of the blues. He also
advanced prededicationism, where heaven
was a kind of gated community to keep out
the riff raff.

F E _ _

A C Z B D O

## RELIGIOUS DIVERSITY

- Anglicans sort of wanted an ambivalent God.

- Louis XIV persecuted Astronaunts.

- Mormonism (a.k.a. "Church of the Large Daily Saints") was founded by Joseph Smith after meeting an Angel named Macaroni.

- Islam is a version of Christianity. It was founded when Moslem became tired of the amplitude of sins he found displayed in his neighborhood.

- People discovered that they could be treated differently if they arranged to be born as Unitarians.

GREETINGS, EARTHLINGS

## VATICAN

- The Pope declared himself inevitable. This was a case of altar ego.

- Leo XIII became the first (non-Catholic) to head the Vatican.

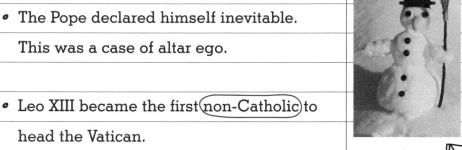

CHRISTIANS INTRODUCED AFRICANS TO SCHOOLS, GOD, AND FROSTY THE SNOWMAN.

- Vatican II was the Pope who served after Vatican I.

- The Catholic church decided that a guilt-line defense was the best offense.

- The Great Schism resulted when one large pope became three somewhat smaller ones.

**Americans created a cornumyopia of new religions. Some of these allowed "speaking in tongues," where people sound like a dog infected with rabbis.**

## THEOLOGY

- Greeks and Pakistanis go to the Eastern Orthodont Church. Unlike Catholics, they did not worship Santa Claus.

- The Catholic and Orthodox churches feature different flavored communion waffles.

- Purgatory was made available for those who weren't quite sure.

**Creationism is the belief system of people who like to go out and create things. Polo Picaso, for example, would be one of your creationists.**

# Philosophy

## The Rule of Thump

AS OFTEN AS NOT, PHILOSOPHY HAS

A CONNECTION TO IDEAS.

## DEFINITIONS

- <u>A priori</u> knowledge is things that you have already prioritized.

- <u>A posteriori</u> knowledge is knowledge that you learn while sitting down.

- <u>Heuristics</u> lays down the rule of thump. This applies when the elements of a problem come together like pieces of a puzzle that could not be put together.

- <u>Inductive and deductive</u> logic are two different ways of gaining logic through ductive ways. Inductive reasoning usually involves electricity.

# 17TH CENTURY

- Unfortunately, the seventeenth century introduced new ideas.

- Descartes began this by stating, "I think, therefore I'm Sam."

- Thomas Hobbes created natural laws.

- Leviathan Hobbes thought that life was nasty, prudish, and short.

**In his best-selling book, Tabula Rasa, Locke taught that man was born as a blank sheep.**

EL SOCRATES.
de
A. BIJUR.

DEEP WITHIN THE DEPTHS OF HISTORY LIVED THREE GREAT AND WISE PHILOSOPHERS OF ANCIENT GREECE. SOCRATES WAS THE FIRST TO USE HORIZONTAL IDEAS. PLATO DID HIS THINKING IN THE CAVE OF AL GORE. ARISTOTLE CONCLUDED FROM THIS THAT PLATO'S TRAIN OF THOUGHT WAS LATE ARRIVING AT THE STATION.

MORE DEFINITIONS

✳ Eschatology is the study of snails. →

✳ Ontology is the study of onts and their moral meaning.

✳ Christology can be described as the science of swearing.

✳ Rationalism means calm thinking.

✳ Epistimologists treat skin conditions.

Volare fathered the Enlightenment. Reason cursed through the synex of the European brain. This was a time when everyone had at least one idea, good or bad. The salons of Paris became a zone where individuals were permitted to touch one another in ways otherwise prohibited.

## GREAT THINKERS

- Kant was a metamucilist who taught that we should justify behavior by precisely locating the categorical whatever.

- Comte just said "no" to metal physics.

- Kierkegaard authored Fear of Trampling.

- Nietzsche, who was famous as a sack religionist, can be seen as a useful antidote to truth.

- Nietzsche frequently exposed himself to Richard Strauss. $\longrightarrow$

Hegel began life as a young Hegelian. His idea was that history was a struggle between thesis and prosthesis. Eventually Hegel was recognized as a dialectical super model. Dialectics, of course, is just one problem creating another problem. Marx later put the diacritical frosting on Hegel's system.

Transcendentalism was a movement to unite the United States with a system of railroads. Emerson became the American Transincidentalist.

Their are many interesting ideas in the twentieth century if we could find some.

W
e
weekend
k
e
n
weekend

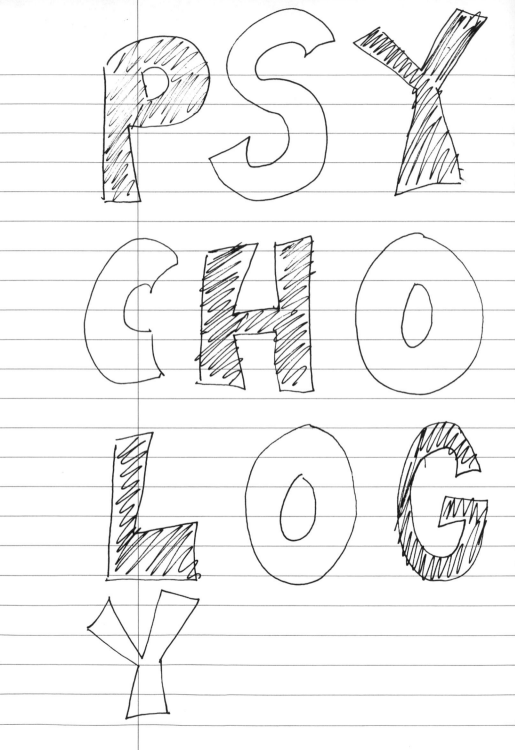

# Psychology
## Neutering Mothers

MOST PSYCHOLOGISTS BELIEVE THAT HUMAN BEHAVIOR
IS CONTROLLED BY SUPERNATURAL FORCES. WE CAN
UNDERSTAND THIS CONCEPT BETTER IF WE THINK
OUTSIDE IN A BOX.

FREUDIAN SLIPS

✳ **Eggmont Freud discovered sex.**

✳ Schadenfreude was Freud's maiden name.

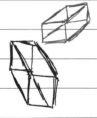

✳ Jung recommended that we appreciate our inherited tendencies by remaining unconscious.

Researchers once thought maturation had more to do with intelligence than neutering, but the role of neutering is seen more in the mothers of today.

## CHILD DEVELOPMENT

- A baby normally prefers its mother's womb to that of a stranger.

- Three infant abilities are heart rate changes, imitation, and facials.

- Infants recognize their mothers voices by measuring their heart rate.

IN CASES
OF SEVERE
DEPRESSION THE
PATIENT BLOTS
OUT THE WORLD
AND ASSUMES A
FECAL POSITION.

Compulsive behavior is a sign of anal relentless personality and can cause people to keep cleaning their house to avoid Germans.

Some people do not cope well. This copulation problem can lead to heroine or alchohol abuse. Alcoholism may involve drinking.

## SEXUALITY

- Most people are either straight, gay, or thespian.

- A part of every population will be bye sexual.

- Intersexuals are people who have sex with themselves instead of others.

- Males who are sexually attracted to their mothers display an Edifice complex. These men never finish prudery.

## DEFINITIONS

- <u>Telepathy</u> is a condition linked by scientists to excess cell phone use.

- <u>Melancholia</u> is allargy to melons.

- <u>Acrophobia</u> is fear of acrobats.

- Xenophobia is fear of xenophones.

- People with <u>triskaidekaphobia</u> are afraid to eat triskats.

*Blah Blah Blah...*

**Extraterrestrial perception, also known as ESPN, lets some people see the future. It is something like women's intermission.**

MORE DEFINITIONS

✳ Multiple personality disorder occurs when a person comes into contact with too many people.

✳ Alienation is the nation someone else comes from.

✳ Transference is where we spread our problems onto others.

✳ Anal stimulation can lead to obsessive propulsive disorder.

**Bi-polar disorder is a disease suffered by Arctic explorers. It is twice as bad as unipolar disorder.**

## SCHIZOPHRENIA

- Symptoms of schizophrenia include thought broadcast.

- Schizophrenics may become catatonic, which means that they move like statues.

## TREATMENT

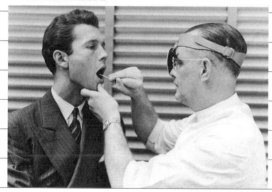

- Many emotional disturbences can be treated by swallowing a couple of suppositories and seeing the doctor in the morning.

TWENTIETH-CENTURY CONFLICT HAS CAUSED SEVERAL INFECTIOUS MENTAL DISEASES. MANY VETERANS OF WORLD WAR ONE WERE SHUNNED AND LEFT TO DEAL WITH THEIR SHELL SHOCK, NOW KNOWN AS POST PARTUM DEPRESSION.

- Simple phobias can be cured when the subject is made to understand that his problem is basically self-dilution. One way to accomplish this is by drowning the patient.

- Munchausen's syndrome is a psycho-semantic problem and can be cured by prescribing a placenta.

**More serious diseases used to be treated with shock therapy, where the patient was placed in an electric chair and repeatedly electricuted. This typically made the patient numb and happy. Those of us privileged to live in the twenty-fifth century know better.**

# Music

## With a Song in Our Hair

THE THREE GREAT "B"s OF MUSIC ARE BOCK,
BATOGAN AND BRONZE.

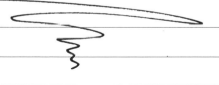

## HIGH NOTES

✳ Sound began in Ancient Greece.

✳ Melody was based on systems known as Lydian, Mixologist, Frigid and Diabetic.

✳ Music at Jewish services included playing on the chauffeur.

Bach's scared choral music includes the B Minor Mess and a Passion based on the gospels of Matthew and Mary. He was also responsible for Torcal and Fudge. The Well Tempered Cavalier changed keyboard music forever. Bach was a very proliferate composer and all one million of his famed works can be found in his BMW. He had over one hundred children and was, of course, very famous for work with his organ. Two of his succesfull sons were Jesus Christ Bach and Bacherini.

As a prodigious child, Wolfgang Annapolis Mozart would play the violin upside down while his father would company him on the clamourcord. Mozart wrote The Attack from the Cerebellum, Cutie Fan Tootie, and Marriage of Fellatio. Some of these have an Italian libido. Unfortunately, Mozart had to compose his Requiem posthumusly.

Ludwig and Beatoven were two composers who highlited the 1700s. Sadly, Beetoven became hearing impaled about halfway back through his career. He composed several light pieces known as baguettes and the Erotica Symphony.

THE EARLY CHURCH MADE MUCH USE OF CANT. THIS WAS A FORM OF CHORAL MONOTONY.

The "celebrated five" composers of the Russian school were Mussolini, Rimsky-Korstakov, Borotone, Sneezy, and Grumpy.

Tchaikovsky composed Al Dente Crockodile. This, however, was the moment when Russian ballet blasted its way into the mainstream. One example was Thaikovsky's Ball Breaker, which appears to have been his idea of enertainment for children.

## OPERA

- Hudini's opera Madame Butterball is about an American sailor named Pinsky who meets a Vietnamese girl.

- Handel was half German, half English and half Alsatian. Thus he was very large. His operas were among the first ones to feature female preformers titled "Purina Dona." Male calamari also continued to perform as sopranos for a time.

- As an anti-semite, Richard Wagner of course detested French people and showed this in his work. This is really obvious in the operas that belong to the Lord of the Rings.

The Great American Opera is Gershlynne's Porky Is Best. Gerschwin often composed while under the influence of jazz and electrical impulses. His best known work is Rap Soda and Blues. A cerebral hemroyd required Geschwin's early death. He later became a brand of bicycle.

IGOR!

Igor Stravinsky's dance music was a major cause of World War I.

## MODERN MUSIC

- Dixieland is a song with impossiblizations.

- Unlike jazz, rock and roll conjures up images of heroine that suggest abuse of alcohol and helucinejnic drugs. I can feel the vibrations. There's a song in my hair.

ROCK AND ROLL!

## DEFINITIONS

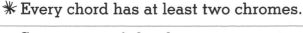

✳ Every chord has at least two chromes. Some <u>types of chords</u> are major, minor, acute and chronic.

✳ The symbol <u>pp</u> stands for "pee twice."

✳ A <u>leitmotif</u> is a motif that doesn't way much.

✳ A <u>canticle</u> is like an icicle only upside down.

✳ <u>Pianoforte</u> was an Italian man who was the inventor of the piano.

✳ The <u>requiem</u> is music sung by the dead.

# Art

## Pigment of the Imagination

ARTISTS OFTEN BEAT A DIFFERENT DRUMMER.

HISTORY

✳ Art forms began during the Paleolithic era with cave paintings and small nomadic sculptures. Cycladic art was inspired by Picasso.

QUEEN

✳ Egyptian artists were required to work sideways from back to front.

✳ Female images in Egyptian sculpture include Queen Hatshepsut, who gained fame by locating Baby Jesus in the bullrushes.

✳ Greek architecture could be Doric or Ironic.

✳ Rome was built in a day. Homes came with garden moratoriums. Amazing aqua ducks supplied fresh water.

Medeval artists were not allowed to know who they were. One example of this is (Anonymous Bosch.)

For some reason, the altar was a major focus of attention in medieval cathedrals. The church apes normally formed a semi-circle around it. The ribbed vault developed as a place where the Pope hid his jewels. Abbot Suger used the pole vault to build higher churches. This gave the Holy Spirit room to zoom.

## RENAISSANCE

- Depth persuasion was all the rage.

- Painters discovered the varnishing point.

- Sculptors visited new dimensions.

- Breughel the Younger became Breughel the Elder.

- Michaelangelo, who wanted to see it as he saw it, had the common sense to get David to pose for him.

- Fresco was a popular snack food supplied by the church.

**Baroque art is noted for golden scrolls, soft clouds, and fat little cheroots.**

ARTISTS

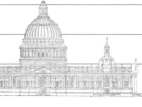

✳ Christopher Robin built St. Paul's.

✳ Giotto illustrated St. Francis of Mississippi.

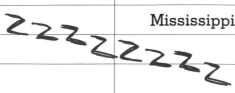

✳ Botticelli made the first moving pictures.

✳ Van Eyck painted The Marriage of Arnold Feeney.

✳ Rubens was enameled with posturesque females.

✳ Rembrandt was Norway's gift to art. His Bathsheba in the Bathroom stunned the artgoing public.

Unfortunately, eighteenth-century painters had to live in the eighteenth century. Delacroix followed his instincts even when he should have left them alone. An example of this is Greece Perspiring on the Dunes.

## IMPRESSIONISM

- Impressionism took Paris under its arms and stroked it until it blushed.

- Monet did not like to paint indoors and so would sit with his weasel in nature.

- Too Loose Latreck could be found at work in cafes and brassieres throughout Paris.

- Van Gogh completed intriguing self-portraits of himself and others.

- Mary Cassat was the only American woman of her time.

- Degas specialized in belly dancers. →

## MORE ARTISTS

✴ After he moved to Maine Winslow Homer traded society ladies for fish and manly men.

~~RAT~~

~~TRA~~

ART

✴ Turner painted marine scenes because he was in the Marines. His later work is mostly pigment of the imagination.

✴ <u>Chagall is hard to</u> understand because he painted in Russian.

✴ Picasso painted Glasnost to show the brutality of it all.

✴ Jackson Potluck is the birth father of splash art.

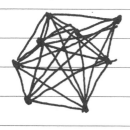

## EVEN MORE ARTISTS

✴ Diego Rivera lived with Frito the Mexican Lady.

✴ Georgia O'Keeffe went to New Mexico in order to paint people at the beach.

✴ Art Deco designed the Chrysler building.

✴ Alexander Calder built mopeds for the ceiling.

✴ Henry Moore specialized in blobs.

**Minimalism produces very small art. It is the opposite of maximalism.**

Cubism is art from Cuba.

**Dadaism is the fathering of illegible children.**

# English
# Literature

## Seminole Works

THE STUDY OF LITERATURE IS VALUABLE BECAUSE
IT ALLOWS US TO IMAGINE DOING CERTAIN KINDS
OF THINGS WITHOUT GETTING CAUGHT AT
REALLY DOING THEM.

PILGRIMS?

Even today a few people have heard of Chaucer. It is, however, a little known fact that he did not know a word of English. Canterbury Tales is about pilgrims on their way to Thanksgiving. This was Chaucer's seminole work. Another promenent mideval author is The Wife of Bath.

Dryden worked closely with Virgil to produce the Aeneid.

Frigidity was the only acceptable literary style in Puritan England. This fact certainly explains Milton. The Restoration was a welcome event, because it allowed the people to resume antics as usual.

Shakespeare won the Nobel prize on several occasions. This makes you a nobel and involves being nightied by the Queen. It is very cool that Shakespere decided to set Richard III in Nazi Germany.

CHARACTERS

✳ MacBeth, being himself, had a problem. He also never overcame the fact that he was Irish.

✳ Ophelia was a victim of teenaged bucolia. The main problem she encountered was that wherever she went, there she was.

✳ Henry V is about a king named Richard III.

✳ Richard III is shown as a hunchback because he always went with his hunches.

✳ The shipwrecked characters in The Tempest remain in a state of confusion induced by a form of mal de merde.

## AUTHORS

❋ William Blake, who was very much his own cosmetologist, was animator of Burn, Tiger, Burn.

❋ Kipling was born first in India and then later in England. He was able to successfully write children's literature as he had been a former child himself.

**Jane Austen's novels are about love, family, and interpersonal enemas. Most of today's Jane Austin afflictionados seem to be women with time in their hands.**

The first major work by an American author is The Holy Bible. ⟶

## ROMANTIC POETRY

- The concept of Romanticism was introduced by Romans studying English literature. Byron became King of the Rowmatics. His poem about Julia Child and the Pilgrims was extreamly popular.

- Keats frequently downloaded his emotions on an unsuspecting public.

- Wollworth's "Tinkerbell Abby" is a good illustration of the struggle between sense and reason.

IRONY IS HOW THE CHARACTERS IN A STORY SHOW THEMSELVES ABLE TO IRON OUT THEIR DIFFERENCES.

- Poetic metre is used to measure the length of a poem. A short one would be less than one meter.

Whitman's poem "Lilacs" deals with the death of President Kennedy. Whitman was very effective in this because he was in the Civil War, which featured several deaths as part of its action. Leaves of Grass was Whitman's attempt to come to terms with substance abuse issues in the 1960s.

Edith Wharton wrote about the Plateau Rich. Her novel House of Mirth exposed a system that forced women to marry into a descent life. Set on Hudson Bay, it is the story of Lily Barth, who was caught revolving somewhere between the upper and middle classes as she searched for some repulsive men to marry.

| | |
|---|---|
| AN EXAMPLE | MAJOR WORKS |
| OF LITERATURE | ✳ An epic is like a docudrama, but more |
| AS SOCIAL | boring. |
| COMMENTARY | |
| IS THACKERY'S | ✳ Great Expectations was a novel Dickens |
| NOVEL VANITY | wrote that was about the time when he |
| FAIR. THIS BOOK | was expecting. |
| UNFORTUNATELY | |
| REQUIRES LESS | ✳ In his play Cliff Notes, George Barnard |
| ATTENTION | Shaw illuminates social issues that |
| DEFICIT THAN | would not be so easily exploded in other |
| IS NOW THE CASE. | medians. |

✳ Teepus Elliot's poem "Hollow Men" is an
important window into this time, because
it is about men who became hollow.

✳ In his popular autobiography,
The Importance of Being Ernest,
Hemmingway tells us what it is like to
live as a man.

* Young David Copperfield was raised by a kind and gentle mother who beat him savagely when she felt like it.

* Jay Gatsby moved to East Egg because it would be a good place to raise chickens.

* The Grapes of Wrath portrays the sufferings of the dust boulders. These poor characters are eventually forced to eat the grapes of wrath one after the other.

* George Sand was the synonym of Blanche Dubois, who freed herself from the constrictions of her times by frequently escaping into men's trousers.

* Brave New World deals with life on planet Moon.

In Isherwood's novel, The Last of Mr. Norris, it is shown how Germany made many advances in the area of sexual preference. The result was people who felt themselves more freely. This idea is also discussed by To the Lighthouse author Vagina Woolf.

## MODERN AMERICAN WRITERS

- As a Southern writer, Eudora Welty was on the inside looking at the outside looking at the inside.

- Faulkner located Yucktabella county on the Gulf coast of Alaska to share his insite into the south.

- Like most modern novels, The Color Purple begins with Chapter Three.

# Language

## Rope Learning

EVERY SENTENCE MUST HAVE A SUBJECT

AND A PREDICAMENT.

KEY TERMS

✳ A diphthong is a very small bottom worn in Brazil.

✳ A morpheme is a phoneme that has given birth to a tiny egglet of meaning.

✳ A sibilant is a venamus reptile.

✳ A fricative is a sound best sounded at a distance from others.

✳ A mangling participle is a sign of poor synapse.

**Around the time of Napoleon all language became French.**

MORE GRAMMAR

✳ The propositional phrase is often an
attempt to answer the questions "where"
and "when"?

✳ In some languages the "t" and "d"
sounds are dental expletives.

✳ Vowell sounds in German can be altered
by placing an omlet on top on them.

✳ The objective case is used when you
want to object to something.

✳ The genital case stands for possession,
because this is something you really
want to keep.

✳ Vocative is for use only in emergency
situations.

THE ONLY WAY
TO UNDERSTAND
INTRANSIGENT
VERBS IS BY ROPE
LEARNING.

## DEFINITIONS

- An <u>acronym</u> refers to spiders.

- A <u>homophone</u> is used in the drum and bungle corps.

- A <u>homonym</u> is a synonym only the other way around.

- A <u>palindrome</u> is a place where the ancient Greeks played basketball.

- <u>Cryptography</u> is the study of graves.

DISTINCTIONS

※ The major differences between Middle English and Modern English resulted from the Great Bowel Shift.

✳ Why would anyone think that Old English is a seperate language? Old people can understand us with no problem if we speak loudly enough.

✳ The main language of the United Kingdom is Arabic.

✳ The fact that Chinese is tonal means that it is best learned by Chinese and musicians.

## MORE DISTINCTIONS

✳ The Maori language differs from the English language because they speak English backward when they speak Maori.

✳ In Japan sentences are literally said backwards.

✳ "Ecce Homo" is Italian for "Look, a Homosexual."

**The two official languages of Canada are Spanish and Canadian. Canada is the third-largest Spanish-speaking country in the world.**

FOOD HAS AN IMPORTANT PLACE IN ITALIAN CULTURE. EVIDENCE FOR THIS IS THE USE OF THE WORD "CHOW" AS A GREETING.

# Ancient & Medieval History

## The Bluebonnet Plague

HISTORY IS A SEARCH FOR PASSED MOVEMENTS.

CULTURES

✳ The Babylonians were able to live only during certain months of the year.

✳ The Assyrians were a ruthless society that would terrorize relentlessly and did so very tactfully.

✳ Hammurabi's Code had hard punishments like having to keep your wife and easy ones like having your ear cut off.

✳ Marriages between the Pharoes and their sisters were used to strengthen family values.

How did Athens and Sparta start out so synomious and then deter themselves to divest in what they became? <u>This is the number one secret of classical iniquity.</u>

**Sparta was a place where men were men and women were men.**

GREEKS & ROMANS

* Athens was ruled by the Airport Council, which enjoyed the right of homicide.

* Thucydides distrusted democracy, because it let sneaky dermatologists take over the goverment.

* Alexander the Great made Greek armies unavoidable. His use of the "phallus" formation was terrifying to enemies.

✳ The Romans easily conquered the Italian peninsula, because it is only six miles long. Their first victims were the Ecuadorians.

✳ The Emperor Constantine moved the capital to Constantinople, probably because he liked the name. After the fall of Rome Constantinople was renamed Timbuctu.

✳ The Edict of Milan made history legal.

✳ Hadrian's Wall protected the English from the Sloths.

blah

blah blah

blah blah

blah

**The fall of Rome was ineffable. The rich lived high with the hogs, dining on tasty and excrable treats. Many found happiness with misery cults. Life became so decadent that people were** commiting chastity **in the streets.**

PEOPLE

✳ Ramses II was famous for being younger than Ramses I.

✳ Pontious Pilot was an official in the Roman Air Force.

✳ Charles Martel won the Tour de France.

✳ Charlemagne was a moonbeam of cultural sensitivity who killed someone only if he or she really disagreed with him.

* Alfred the Great defeated the Great Danes.

* Marco Polo was a popular event in the first Olympics, but was later cancelled due to awkwardness.

* The Ottoman Empire began humbly enough as a group of Turkish tribesmen who enjoyed getting together to massacre their neighbors.

* The people of Africa lived in Africa, but did not yet know this fact.

* Russia discovered that it could be attacked from east, west, up or down.

## ENGLAND

- Three avenues of upward social mobility in Medieval England were wagon, horse, and by foot.

- A vassal was a kind of servant, only rounder.

- The only career option other than peasant was often beggar or village idiot. Some, however, went to town and became gelded craftsmen.

- King John angered his nobles by misplacing France. He was excommunicated by the Pope for this, and thus could not have any more children.

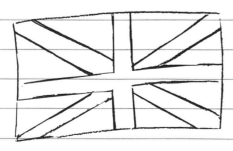

The Middle Ages ended with the Bluebonnet Plague. Rats, fleas, and people lived together and bit each other on a regular basis. It was hard to stay ahead of the grim leaper. The Flatullents were a group that tried to avoid this problem by traveling from place to place wiping themselves. The plague was eventually cured by fleas. When the epidemic was over, there were only a few dozen Europeans left alive. The advantage to this was that people generally had more room.

# Modern European History

## Prancing on Thin Ice

THE PATH TO POWER WAS PAVED WITH GROVEL.

Time was large during the Renaissance. Occasional intellectual activity ocurred even in the Netherlands.

Ivan the Terrible discovered that murder was a good way to kill occasional persons. There was nothing really wrong with this, because Machiavelli states that many famous people have accomplished much while being bad. He mentions, for example, Hannibal Lector and Pope Julius.

## RULERS

- Henry VIII endulged himself in adultery when married and midwifery when not.

- Louis XIV used his glittering balls to attract the nobles of France.

- Peter the Great was a man of enormous projections who moved the capital to St. Peter's Bird. Late in life he was bothered by ticks due to Sysiphus.

I. II. III. IV. V. VI. VIII. IX. X. XI. XII.

Russians at this time were less evolved than other Europeans. Men in Moscow, for example, wore long beards instead of pants. Another one of Russia's problems was minorities like the Poles and Irish.

**The French Revolution was a nice break for everyone.**

TURNING POINTS

\* Nobles who saved themselves by fleeing France during the Revolution are called "French Flies."

\* Napoleon invented the meter, which is used in parking to this day.

＊ 1815 was longer than your usual year.

＊ The Congress of Vienna met in Paris.

＊ Garibaldi headed the Risotto movement.

＊ Queen Victoria married Alfred the Great. ⟶

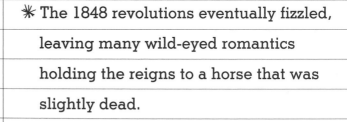

＊ The Franco-Prussian War had a long gesticulation period.

＊ The 1848 revolutions eventually fizzled, leaving many wild-eyed romantics holding the reigns to a horse that was slightly dead.

＊ Kaiser William II wanted Germany to have a place on the Sun, and for this reason kept all his eyes shut to reality.

※ Alfred Dreyfus was framed for selling secrets from his trousseau and sent to Devil's Island, where he was not allowed to go swimming. As a Jewish Catholic, Dreyfus was really isolated.

The Irish Home Rule Bill was a plan to give women equality in the home.

Like a foolishly large and clumsy animal, the force of imperialism stumbled about the world haphazardly raping history. The British Empire reached climax during the age of Queen Cleopatra. The sun never set while the British enjoyed this climax.

**Some of these ideas are unfortunately too long for my attention spam.**

GAVRILO PRINCIP, WHO WAS A MEMBER OF THE BLACKFOOT ORGANIZATION, SHOT PRINCESS FERN. AUSTRIA SENT THE SERBS A SUBLIMATION THEY COULDN'T REFUSE. THIS REQUIRED ALL FUN TO BE IMMEDIATELY CANCELLED.

The European powers began to play scrabble for Africa. King Leopold owned the Belgian Condo personally. (French claims to it remained largely theatrical.) The Boer War started after the discovery of almond mines in Africa. It led to the first gorilla war fair. These empires were exactly like Hitler except for the small difference that they did not exterminate masses of people.

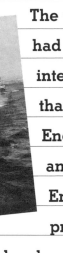

**The Germans built a huge navy, but had no water for it. This started an international dreadlock competition that unwisely threatened the English primate. Britain, France, and Russia formed the Triple Entendre. These conditions produced a dangerous kind of showboatism. The great powers were prancing on thin ice.**

# American History

## Business Unusual

THE STUDY OF HOW HISTORY IS WRITTEN
IS CALLED HISTRIONICS.

The Norse were in North America before Columbus, because they followed the camels they raised in Asia. Lief Eriksson was the first explorer to reach Graceland. In 1492 Columbus established the New World, also known as the United States. He brought back written language and Havoc. Havoc is a disease which spread all over the New World.

New England was founded by people fleeing religious percussions. The Pilgrems, for example, were Jewish refugees. Most English colonists could not speak Spanish, so it was difficult for them to hear what the Indians were trying to say to them.

Thomas Paine thought the problem with monarchy was that it tended to rely too much on having a king.

King George suffered from a uterine disorder known at the time as The Blues. This caused him to drop his marbles one by one. After the Seven Ears War British soldiers stood around while Americans buried the dead bodies. For this reason Americans opposed a standing army. The Stamp Act enraged Americans because it banned stamp collecting.

California was first settled by the Chinese, a fact that explains names like "Los Angeles." The Spanish conveniently located their missions along Interstate 5. This was the famed El Casino Real.

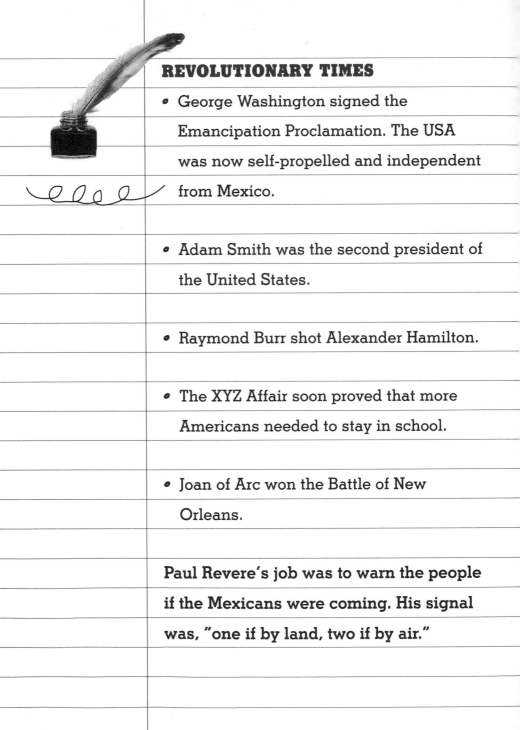

## REVOLUTIONARY TIMES

- George Washington signed the Emancipation Proclamation. The USA was now self-propelled and independent from Mexico.

- Adam Smith was the second president of the United States.

- Raymond Burr shot Alexander Hamilton.

- The XYZ Affair soon proved that more Americans needed to stay in school.

- Joan of Arc won the Battle of New Orleans.

Paul Revere's job was to warn the people if the Mexicans were coming. His signal was, "one if by land, two if by air."

The Mayflower Compact was a small boat carried on the Mayflower for use in case of emergency.

## TO THE CIVIL WAR

* The Missouri Compromise was when Missouri said it would agree to half of everything. It led to the Kansas-Alaska Act.

* Pickett's Charge was a famed case of credit card fraud.

* James K. Polk invented the polka dot.

✳ President Lincoln was shot in his Ford.

✳ Slavery was the big issue in the Anti-Bedlam South.

✳ Wilmot Proviso was a slave who led a revolt.

✳ John Brown was a radical abortionist who hoped that Harper's Fairy would aid him.

✳ Jim Crow was an African-American civil rights leader.

The Civil War was caused by the Articles of Confederation. The South had generals like Lee and Longfellow. Stonewall Jackson was his own horse until he died of a moral wound. Sherman announced that, "War is swell." The Civil War was ended by the Marshall Plan.

Capitalism encroached on the nation, nuzzling it with venturesome forepaws. This was the age of the Robber Bears. Andrew Carnegie was the King of Steal. Comrade Vanderbuilt tried to fleas the American consumer.

THE UNDERGROUND RAILROAD WAS BUILT AS THE NATION'S FIRST PUBLIC TRANSIT SYSTEM.

## KEY PEOPLE

- William Randoph Hearse placed his organ at the disposal of imperialists.

- Grover Cleveland lost an election when it became known that he fathered Babe Ruth.

- Otto von Bismarck represented North Dakota in the US Senate.

- Teddy Roosevelt promised everyone a progressive Square Meal.

After World War I Americans just wanted to return to business unusual. <u>The New Deal legalized gambling.</u> Franklin Delmonico Rosevelt used the Civilian Confiscation Corps to solve the Depression. When challenged, he responded by pecking the Supreme Court. The United States entered World War Two after the Vietnamese bommed Pearl Harbor.

THE STATUE OF LIBERTY WAS A GIFT TO THE AMERICAN PEOPLE FOR THE SERVICES OF THE TUSKEGEE AIRMEN.

KEY EVENTS

✳ The G.I. Bill required all veterans to take medical examinations.

✳ Reagan won the Nixon-Kennedy debate.

✳ JFK was assassinnated by Mexican spy Lee Harley Osborn.

✳ Barry Goldwater hosted a popular TV show for kids.

* Timothy Leary burned down Chicago, but he did not mean to.

* The Manhattan Project introduced public housing to New York City.

* Winston Churchill founded the NAACP.

* Jay Eager Hoover built the Hoover Dam.

* America's principal adversaries in World War II were Russia and China.

* Dwayne D. Ikenhowitzer was President of the fifties.

* The Civil Rights Act of 1964 gave equal rights to civilians.

**The Watergate Scandal was when there was not enough water in the nation's capital. Nixon knew about this and did not care.**

NIXON

Richard Nixon gamboled with the nation's future. The Watergate Committee investigated a plot by Russian spies to take control and spoil some of President Nixon's plans. Nixon's main problem was misclosure of facts he continued to hide. The Warren Commission finally forced him to abscond.

## MORE PEOPLE

✳ Jimmy Carter was elected as President after Nixon because he was viewed as partially rational.

✳ President Reagan started "Good Morning America."

✳ Bill Clinton was impeached for invalid sexual activities.

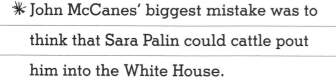

✳ During his first term George W. Bush was interested mostly in the weather.

✳ John McCanes' biggest mistake was to think that Sara Palin could cattle pout him into the White House.

# The Modern World

## The Beer Hall Pooch

IT IS A MAJOR PROBLEM THAT HISTORY ALWAYS

KEEPS HAPPENING.

Germany started World War I with about 900,000,000 soldiers. France had 50 or so and thus the sides were a little uneven. The Schlieffen Plan was Germany's idea to surprise the French by blowing up Berlin beforehand.

Life in the trenches was very dangerous due to constant attacks by submarines.

## WAR

- World War II began when Hitler decided that he would like to visit Paris. Suddenly it was VD Day in Europe. Hitler, who had begun as a painter, wound up painting himself into a corner.

- Japan faced total aliteration. America dropped the nucular bomb on Nicaragua. This was a very large surprise for the Japanese.

- The Lusitania was sunk by a Japanese iceberg.

- The Spanish Influenza eliminated Spain.

- The Irish Free State was a place where everything was free.

- The Dawes Plan let Germany pay its debts excrementally.

- The Axis powers, who were Germany, Russia, and Israel, united in 1936.

- The Maginot Line was a 1940s dance craze.

- Stalin announced himself to be dead in his post-mortem speech.

- Nikita Khrushchev was the daughter of an Air Force officer.

- During the Cold War Berlin was divided by the Wailing Wall. The Allies supplied Berlin with food by telephone.

- Fidel Castro turned Canada into a Communist country.

- President Carter signed the Salt and Salt-Free Treaties with the Russians.

College in a Nutskull

- Brezhnev's most impressive accomplishment might have been his death in 1982.

- Hamas is an Isrealy leader who refuses to remove his sediments from the bank.

The Balkans continue to be very inappropriate. The region is like a mince meat pie where the raisins don't like the meat and the mince wants to kill the fruity bits. Ethnic clenching spelled "The End" for Yugoslavia. This was another case of old whine in new bottles.

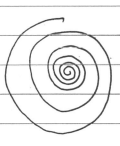

**The search for peace in the Gaza Strip failed because both sides do their forwards thinking while looking backwards.**

# Government

## Dude Process

DEMOCRACY IS A SYSTEM WHERE PEOPLE ARE

RULED BY A KING.

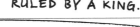

The three branches of American government are President, Church, and State.

## CONGRESS

- The houses of the federal legislature are Senate, House, and Congress.

- The House of Resentatives is the largest branch of feral government. It has 365 members, or one for every voter.

- The Majority Leader is also President Per Diem of the Senate.

- Congress does not have the power to make law. Laws are invented by the courts.

- Bicameralism is where cameras are prohibited from the courtroom. Unicameralism has now been completely decriminalized.

## EXECUTIVE BRANCH

- The executive branch exists because Congress allows it to exist.

THE SECRETARY OF STATE IS IN CHARGE OF THE STATES.

- The President appoints the secretaries and the govenors.

- The Attorney General is Commander of the Army and Head of the Joined Chiefs.

- The Press Secretary keeps the media at bait.

**Checks and balances are what the police do to catch drunk drivers.**

## JUDICIAL BRANCH

- Every person has the right to a Jersey Trial. This is part of dude process.

- Common law is for the common people.

- Case law is law that is stored in a case.

- Habeas corpus states that any deceased person must be returned to their point of origin and relatives.

- Questions of heredity go to Prostate Court.

**Felonies are crimes that we might sometimes want to committ, but the better part of deception tells us not to. Middle-sized crimes are known as mister meaners. They are more serious than little stuff like mooning cars from the team bus.**

CONSTITUTION
※ The United States Constitution promises public tranquilization to all.

✳ The Fifth Amendment contains information about intimate domain and gives us the right not to intimidate yourself.

✳ The Eight Amendment bans cool and unusual punishment.

✳ The Fifteenth Amendment is unconstitutional.

✳ The Eighteenth Amendment enforced prostitution.

## GOVERNMENTAL AGENCIES

• The Park Service is a big fat example of government waste. Citizens don't need the government telling them where to park!

• The Department of the Interior deals with our private areas.

- The Census Bureau takes the cense of the country.

- Burrocracy is rule by burros.

ENGLISH GOVERNMENT

＊ Great Britain has a paramilitary system of government.

＊ The Prime Minister heads the Church of England.

＊ Since all Americans emigrated from England our goverments are similar.

The Magna Carta gave women the vote; and Margaret Thatcher proudly signed it into law.

## CANADA

Canada lacks a formal system of government. The Canadian Constitution is based on the British North African Act, which gave the country a parliament to mock the one in Britain. Canadian citizens are therefore simultaneous British suspects. The motto of Canada is "Peace, Order, and Goods for the Government."

*eh?*

## POLITICS IN CANADA

- When no party has a majority in parlament, the leaders get together to form a collision government.

- The Senate of Canada is a place where older politicians are sent to expire before they can do any more harm.

- The Minister of External Affairs polices the Prime Minister's love life.

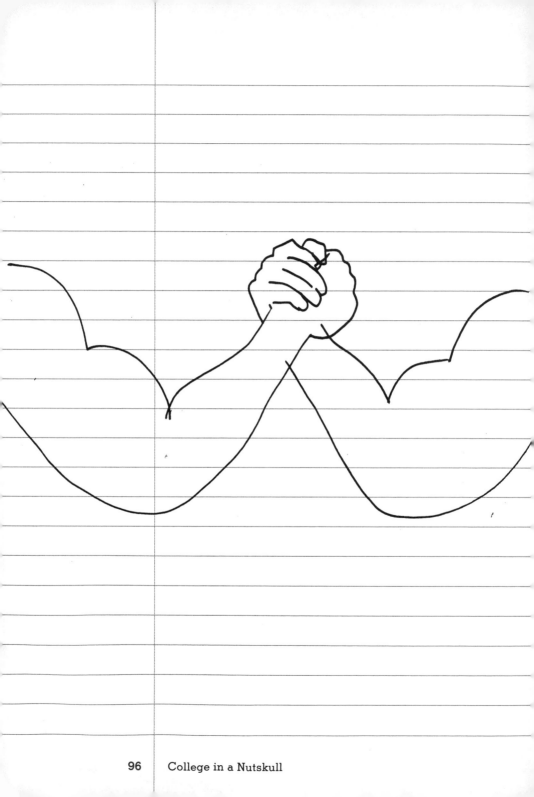

# Political Science

## A Night at the Revolution

POLITICAL THEORY HELPS US TO AVOID GETTING TOO
CAUGHT UP WITH REALITY.

Marx got his dialect from Hegel. An inherent problem in Marx's thinking is that it is too hard to grasp the concepts. This is because Marx thought one thing, but his mind thought another thing. When the revolution failed to put in an appearance, he moved to America and made old movies with his brothers. Toward the end of his life Marx could be described as a recovering Communist.

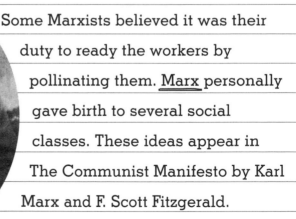

Some Marxists believed it was their duty to ready the workers by pollinating them. Marx personally gave birth to several social classes. These ideas appear in The Communist Manifesto by Karl Marx and F. Scott Fitzgerald.

## AFTER MARX

✳ During the twentieth century socialism
went from a group of ideas heated up in
a crackpot on the back burner to one that
took over the whole kitchen.

✳ The theory of permanent revolution was
when revolution was seen as an endless
night out on the town.

✳ The real trouble started when Lenin
alloued Stalin to have his finger in too
many eyes.

✳ Trotsky wanted to spread the revolution
like butter with his propaganda, but didn't
see that the butter was hard to spread
because Russia is such a cold place.

RONALD REAGAN
COULD BE
DESCRIBED AS A
CONSERVATIVE
BECAUSE HE LIVED
FAR AWAY AND
LONG AGO.

## RIGHT ON

- A conservative is a person with a detailed interest in our behind.

- Edmund Burke believed that experience was the best hope for futility.

- Some French conservatives were once so unhappy that they decided to move to another century.

## LEFT OVERS

- Most liberals are circular humanists. They want to help the government by disorganizing it. This has been there acrylic heel.

- Socialism is like when you go out with your friends.

- Fascism is where your social life is totally on Facebook.

**Public opinion is not rational, because people base their opinion on logic.**

TWO PARTY SYSTEM

✳ The two main American parties today are the Yankees and the Confederates.

✳ The symbol of the Republicans is the bull.

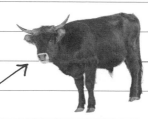

✳ The symbol of the Democrats is a bear.

**Blue states are where people go when they feel depressed.**

**Red states are the warmer states.**

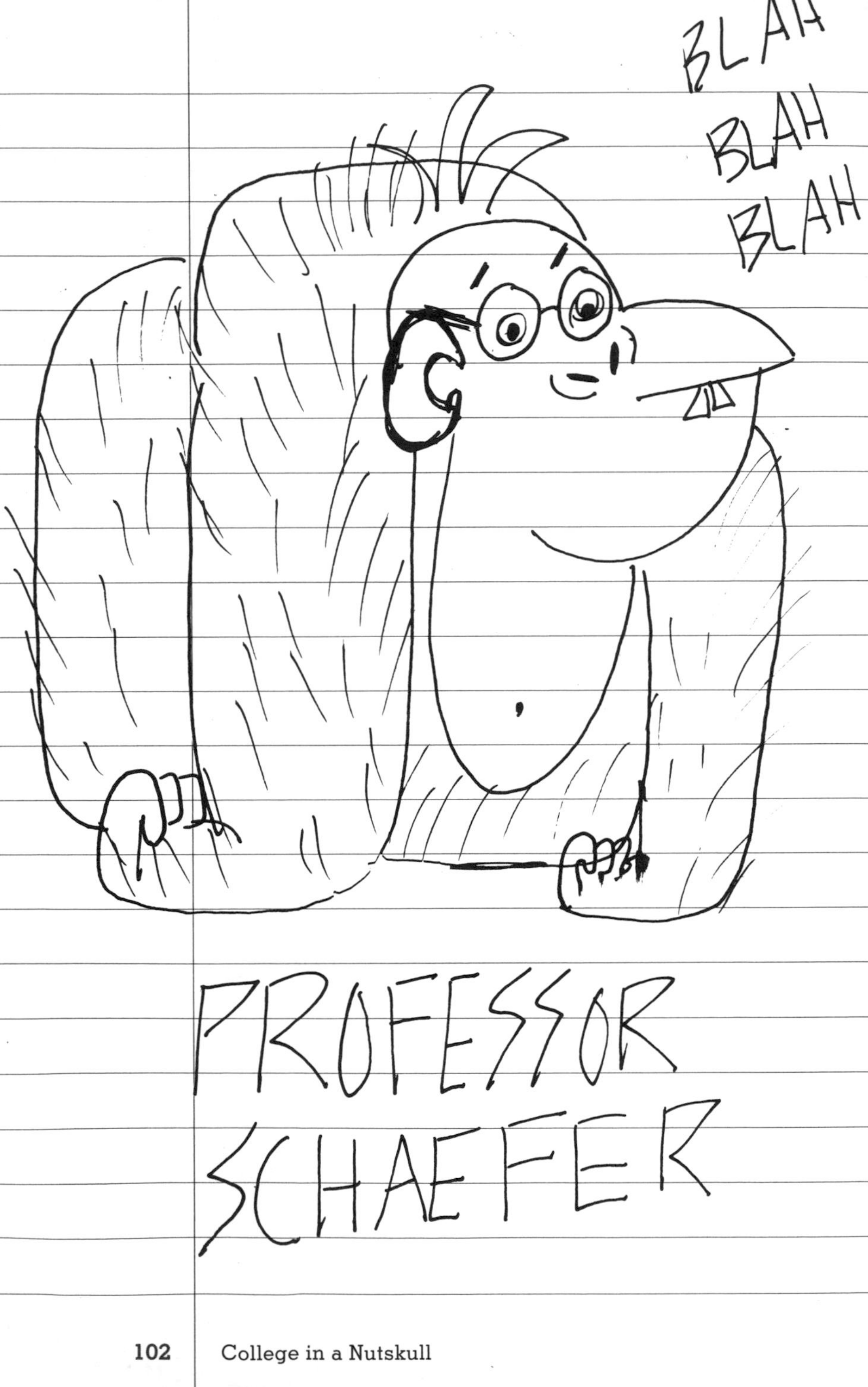
BLAH
BLAH
BLAH
PROFESSOR
SCHAEFER

# Anthropology & Sociology

## Upherd Mobility

DARWINISM IS THINKING LIKE AN APE.

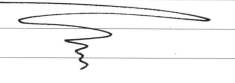

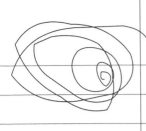

## DEFINITIONS

- <u>Cultural relativism</u> is culture that is passed down by relatives.

- <u>Anthropology</u> is the study of outer space.

- <u>Sociology</u> is the study of sociologists.

- <u>Typology</u> is a theory that has helped typists around the world.

ABGD

- <u>Social Darwinism</u> was Darwin's wife. They had a good relationship and many children, but she did not share his interest in animals and others.

Between 400,000 BC and 7,000 BC Barbarians emerged as the first life forms. Thesaurus Rex walked the earth, munching as he went. These were antidelusional times.

## KEY PEOPLE

* Random Sample was the original Social Scientist and used to be a professor at Harvard.

* Verstehen was a famous German sociologist.

* The pre-Cambrian Era was the era before the Cambrians arrived.

Unlike the inhabitants of Africa that had a culture, the Maori did not. Europeans were thus able to bribe the Maori with materials foreign to them, such as orgasms and ideas.

The main dietary staple in pre-Columbian South America was manic root. This kept the people happy, fed, and very active.

NATIVE AMERICANS

❋ The vast majority of Native Americans are Hindus.

❋ The Mayans worshipped on the sun.

❋ The Incas were a group of peaceful vegetarians whose only slight weakness was the odd human sacrifice.

The bourgeoisie reached their place in the sun during the nineteenth century, but they were not able to enjoy it long enough to get a tan.

## CLASS DIFFERENCES

- The middle class is normally found in the middle of a country.

- Poverty is caused by not having wealth.

- Upherd mobility in America is not as easy as you might think.

- In the 1950s many middle class Americans fled the inner cities to the suburbs in order to escape from tornadoes.

- The working class is the only social class that has men, women, and children in it.

## RACIAL MIX

AMERICA'S POPULATION IS ONE-QUARTER HISPANICS, ONE-QUARTER AFRICAN-AMERICANS, ONE-QUARTER NON-HISPANIC WHITES, ONE QUARTER NATIVE AMERICANS, ONE QUARTER ASIANS, AND ONE QUARTER OTHERS.

America is the melting pod, where alien life forms can be exchanged for something better. The United States received Europe's populous, processed them, and spit them out into the country. Hoards passed through (Elvis Island.) In order to be successful, immigrants had to forget who they were and American-size themselves.

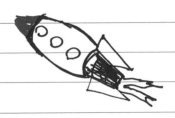

# Economics

## Grosser National Products

THE THEORY OF SURPLUS VALUE IS MARX'S IDEA THAT
YOU ALWAYS SHOP WITH COUPONS.

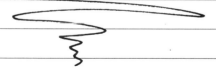

## DEFINITIONS

- Supply-side economics is where everybody has lots of supplies.

- Dependency theory is about how to suck others dry.

- Capitalism is an economic system in which one company is in complete control. It was developed in Russia by Marx and Inglas.

- Compound interest is the interest from more than one loan.

- Sublime rate mortgages turned out to be less than a wise idea.

GOAL!!!

The goal of all bankers is to become transparent so they cannot be seen getting into trouble.

Two variables effect exchange rates. These are store policy and the goods you want to return.

## MORE DEFINITIONS

✻ A limited liability company is a business where you don't have to take responsibility for things.

✻ Oligopoly is the generic brand of Monopoly.

✻ The Standard and Poors Index draws the poverty line.

✻ The AFL-CIO was the first professional football league.

✻ One way for a business to cut costs is to <u>reduce the size of the workers</u>.

✳ The Federal Reserve System protects the culture of Native Americans.

✳ The chief products of Iowa are coal and fruits. You can see farmers there riding their huge concubines down the interstate.

The causes of deflation are a bunch of aspects put together. It is more serious than plain flation.

The difference between elastic demand and inelastic demand is that the former is easier to move around.

INTERNATIONAL

✳ NAFTA regulates trade between the USA, Mexico, and Alaska.

✳ Israel is the world's leading oil producer.

✳ The main export of Saudi Arabia has to be sand.

✳ Germany, being a developed country, has a grosser national product than the developing country, Egypt.

✳ After the war Japan suffered from a prostate economy.

✳ The currency of Mexico is the pinyata. ⟶

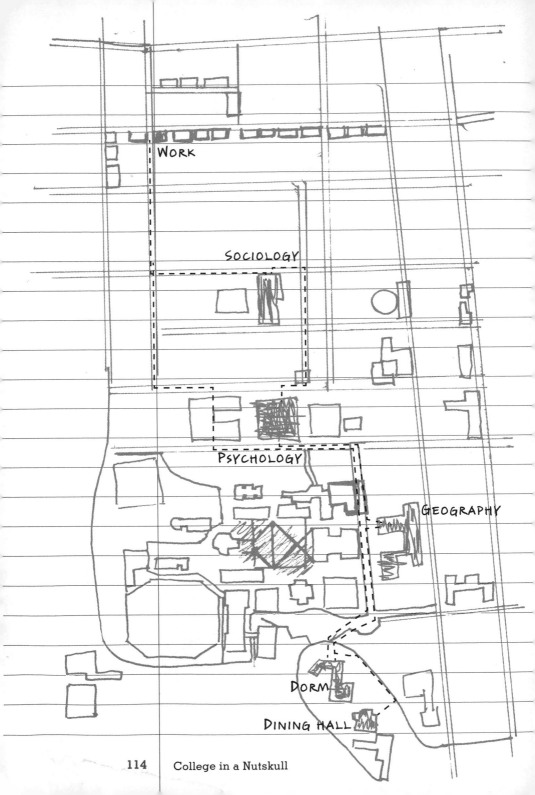

WORK

SOCIOLOGY

PSYCHOLOGY

GEOGRAPHY

DORM

DINING HALL

# Geography

## Out There Somewhere

I STOOD ON THE ALPS AND SAW ARGENTINA.

In the 1800s explorers discovered that the earth was sort of round. If you drew a straight line through the earth from New York it would come out in California. This means that California is the antipathy of New York.

## DEFINITIONS

- The map is divided into lattitude and altitude.

- <u>Longitude is like latitude only longer.</u>

- The Arctic Circle is a dogsled race held every year in Alaska.

- The equator equals everything out.

- Continental drift is when large numbers of Mexicans enter the USA.

- The upside to global warming is that we will finally discover what is buried under the polar ice caps.

**Global warming is a result of too many people becoming closer together.**

NATURAL EVENTS

\* The rain that falls in the desert is usually not very wet.

\* Permafrost is a Russian hair treatment.

\* Sudden, unexpected natural disasters often come as a surprise.

\* <u>Volcanoes explode</u> when the earth has too much stuff in it.

EARTHQUAKES ARE CAUSED BY AGGRESSIVE MOVEMENTS OF THE TEUTONIC PLATES. AT SEA THIS CAN RELEASE A SASHIMI.

* The absence of soil can result in low crop yields. The Dust Bowl, however, was caused by too much dirt in the soil.

**The potato was first introduced to Europe by McDonald's.**

KEY FACTS

* The United Kingdom is located somewhere out there. It is made up of England, Scotland and Northern Israel.

* The industrial revolution started in England because of the tropical climate there.

* The shape of England is very fluid. The English channel, for example, did not exist until 1313.

* New England is the part of England that is newer.

FACTOID

* The only nation which is also a continent is the United States.

IN THE 1500S JAPAN DECIDED TO BE AN ISLAND IN ORDER TO KEEP AWAY FROM OTHERS.

* Europe is several miles to the right of the USA.

* Argentina's leading farm product is pompous cattle.

* Purdah is a place in Indiana where women live in self-delusion.

* Burma has changed its name to "Miramax".

* Every spring the Nile helps Egypt to soil itself. This is the gift of anal flooding.

CHICAGO IS THE
SECOND LARGEST
CITY ON THE
EAST COAST.
ALL CITIES WERE
MODELED AFTER
CHICAGO. EVEN
THE IDEA OF
A CITY ITSELF
CAME FROM
CHICAGO.

* The Suess Canal connects the Meditaranean to the Pacific.

* Australia is very dry, because it is hard for rain to reach the other side of the world.

* Guadalcanal is a small canal discovered near the Panama Canal.

* Indochina is the part of China where all the Indians live.

| PLACE | CAPITAL CITY |
|---|---|
| Austria | Virginia |
| Canada | Buffalo |
| Malaysia | Copacabana |
| Massachussetts | Cape Town |
| Mexico | New Mexico |
| Puerto Rico | Don Juan |
| Texas | Alamo |

# Science & Technology

## Critical Mess

SCIENCE ADVANCES BY PROVING FALSEHOODS.

Newton invented time and motion. He and his friends also discovered many other new things, like that tomorrow will always follow today.

## NEWTON'S LAWS

- What goes up must come down.

- The weight of something when it falls is twice its weight.

- Every action is equal or opposite.

- All things move at the same time.

- For every action there is something new to avoid.

**The moon is a small ball that rotates the earth. Originally it was a chunklet that broke off from earth. The Grand Canyon is the scar from this.**

## SCIENTISTS

- <u>Copernicus</u> discovered the sun.

- <u>Kepler</u> discovered the earth.

- <u>Galileo</u> visited other planets and got in trouble with the Catholic church.

- Aristotle thought that animals reproduced by spontaneous combustion.

- Pliny the Younger invented the triangle, the rectangle, and the octangle.

- <u>Darwin</u> proved that all <u>people were apes.</u>

## SCIENTIFIC THINKING

✳ Natural selection is when a person shops orgasmically.

✳ Scientists use the Celsius scale to boil water at a lower tempeture. Civilians, however, use the Fairandright degrees.

✳ The discovery of nuclear fizz is an example of how science can change the world. First, of course, you need to achieve critical mess.

✳ Plants have been around almost as long as people.

✳ Thunderheads are bad-tempered clouds.

| | |
|---|---|
| MONDAY | |
| TUESDAY | |
| WEDNESDAY | |
| THURSDAY | |
| FRIDAY | |
| **SATURDAY** | |
| **SUNDAY** | |

✳ A typhoon is a tornado aimed at Asian people.

MEDICAL THINKING

✳ Early doctors performed surgery mainly for their own amusement. Many believed that the body was controlled by the four jokes—hair, blood, water, and fling.

✳ If tissues look confused the patient should have an autopsy before diagnosis.

**Johann Gutenberg invented moveable type so that books could be published all over the place. He also invented the Chinese.**

In 1947 the Russians shocked the world by sending Beatnik into space. Yuri Gagarin became the first human to walk on Mars. America was worried that its mistles had weaker propellers than Russian ones.

The Kennedy Space Center, however, was cleverly located in Florida, which is closer to the Sun that the rest of the country.

WEAPONS OF MASS DESCRIPTION ARE A VERY HUGE THREAT TO OUR PLANET.

MORE DEFINITIONS

✳ The halogen bomb transformed international relations.

✳ What could be scarier than an incontinent ballistic missile?

College in a Nutskull

# RANDOM
# NOTES

PRESIDENT

KENNEDY

ORDERED

A SMALL,

AMBIGUOUS

LANDING AT THE

BAY OF PIGS.

THIS LED TO THE

US TAKEOVER OF

CUBA.

George III was George Washington's birth name.

Sixties hippies used flower powder and other mind-alternating substances to create feelgoodism.

Every Hindu hopes to be eventually reincarnated as Brahms.

The Great Wall was built by the Chinease to keep out the English.

The Boxer Rebellion began the struggle for animal rights.

The Japanese were very wise to avoid involvement in the Russo-Japanese War.

The untouchables are people who are not able to be harmed because of their amazing powers.

Edipus killed his parents before being born and thus set himself up for later stress.

## EXPLORERS

- Europeans expanded themselves as they searched for gold and squirrels.

- Vasco Iguana visited many oceans.

- Balboa invented the Pacific Ocean and later settled there with a group of his friends.

- Hernan Cortes interred Mexico.

- Pizzaro found a piece of Africa that had been lost.

Stalin was just a secretary who wanted more. His power accent began when he inseminated himself into Lenin's good graces.

MATA HARI
WAS A FEMME
FATALITY.

The Neolithic revolution began when man stopped chipping his stones and started polishing his tool to make it last longer. This social transformation included the pasturizing of animals and the beginning of subversive agriculture. Personkind was now dragging her nuckles across a whole new tableau.

## WOMEN'S STUDIES

Gender is something you have. Sex is something you do.

FLORENCE NIGHTINGALE WAS A BIRD AUTHOR AND EXPERT ON ORTHINOLOGY.

Most people have historically been only men, but more social and gender mobility became available after the Second World War.

Traditional societies limit girls to bridle expectations. Families in this system force daughters to merry a man. Such "enraged" marriages can happen before the age of adultery.

During the Middle Ages women became the sole childbearers.

World War One liberated American women from the requirement to wear clothing at all times while outside the home. Women of those times were known as flappers because there things flapped around. Today both men and women are able to dress indiscriminantly.

MORE FACTS

❋ The English Parliament declared women invisible in 1884.

❋ The first countries to give the vote to women were New Zealand and Wyoming.

❋ American women won the right to vote in 1973.

MEDEVAL MEN SAW WOMEN AS SEXUALLY FURIOUS, A FACT WHICH MADE THEM AVOID COMMITMENT WHENEVER POSSIBLE.

✳ Mary Wollstonecraft angered many with her amazing novel, The Vindictive Rights of Woman.

FEMINISTS BELIEVE THAT WOMEN SHOULD HAVE THE SAME RIGHTS AS PEOPLE.

✳ Rosie the Rib Eater and her sisters acquired male tools in the factories of World War Two. The military even allowed some women to fly planes, but only inside the home.

✳ Women are still getting brain dents from head-butting the glass ceiling.

By being intelligent and informed, modern woman can produce even more scholarly inept children. In any case, if mom can raise the kids, then dad is left as little more than conscious fertilizer. Why should anyone be sorry about the end of the thermonuclear family?

# ACKNOWLEDGMENTS

This book took a village to produce. Friends and colleagues showered me with a harvest of material so abundant that only a fraction of it could fit into these pages.

They include Bruce Adams, Keith Alexander, Simone Ameskamp, Joel Best, Sally Brasher, Arne Brekke, V.J. Brown, Pat Byram, Momodou Darboe, Betty Ellzey, John Finnegan, Ethan Fischer, James E. Fox, Guy Frank, Hannah Geffert, Laura Gellot, Tom Goetz, David Gordon, Karen Green, James Greenlee, Max Guirguis, Walter Hanak, Harold Heft, Doug Horner, Chuck Kelly, Stacy Kendig, Frank Kenesson, Linda Kinney, Paul Kreuzer, Pam Lang, Eve Levin, James Madden, Mark Madison, Nick Martin, Tim Meade, Robert R. Miller, James Millward, Tom Panebianco, William Pardus, Rob Parkinson, Tom Patterson, Kenneth Portnoy, Walter Powell, Arthur Preisinger, Claire Robertson, Howard Seiler, Ralph Sherrard, Shaun Skinner, Stephanie Slocum-Schaffer, Mark Snell, Howard Spendelow, John Stealey, Linda Tate, Carolyn Thomas, Jerry Thomas, Bob Willgoos, Denis Woods, Nadine Zimmerli, and several others who have chosen to remain anonymous. Special thanks go to James Dignan and Robert O'Shea of the University of Otago,

who graciously permitted me to mine their website of New Zealand student howlers (http://psy.otago .ac.nz/r_oshea/howlers.html). It was a pleasure to collaborate with Jay Schaefer, whose creative editorial insight informs every aspect of this study guide, and with Ruth Sullivan and the rest of the Workman team. I owe a substantial debt of gratitude to my agent, Daniel Greenberg. My wife, Ann, has been my chief test audience and a constant source of support.

## ABOUT THE AUTHOR

Anders Henriksson is Professor of History at Shepherd University. His first humor book, the bestselling *Ignorance Is Blitz* (originally published as *Non Campus Mentis*), appeared in 2001. His pieces on college student bloopers have been published in *Harper's Magazine* and *The Wilson Quarterly*, and he has been featured on *Today*, *CBS Sunday Morning*, and NPR. He is also the author of numerous publications on modern Russian and Baltic history. Professor Henriksson lives with his wife, Ann, in Harpers Ferry, West Virginia.

# PHOTO CREDITS:

## Great grades for IGNORANCE IS BLITZ,*
## the first book from Professor Anders Henriksson,
## a *New York Times* bestseller

"Glorious! . . . equal opportunity idiocy for every era."
—*The Philadelphia Inquirer*

· · · · · · ·

"A horrifically hilarious compendium . . . knitting together
errors, assumptions, and creative fact-making that are
shocking and hysterical."
—*Associated Press*

· · · · · · ·

"You'll laugh until you cry, shedding tears for the state of
American education."
—*Baltimore Sun*

· · · · · · ·

"Call them malaprops, bloopers, or blunders. The
compilation's display of ignorance is bliss to read—
revisionist history with a vengeance."
—*Capital Times,* **Madison, Wisconsin**

· · · · · · ·

"Very funny."
—*Seattle Times*

· · · · · · ·

"Who knew that history could be so funny and
creatively spelled?"
—*Columbia Dispatch*

· · · · · · ·

"The book is the funniest thing I have come across in ages.
I read it over the phone to my brother last weekend and we
were both on the floor asphyxiated from laughter."
—**Richard Nilesen,** *Des Moines Register*

*Originally published as NON CAMPUS MENTIS.